MW00567375

MONEY
POWER
For
Families

By Tama McAleese
Certified Financial Planner

THE CAREER PRESS
180 FIFTH AVE.
PO BOX 34
HAWTHORNE, NJ   07507
1-800-CAREER-1
201-427-0229 (OUTSIDE U.S.)
FAX: 201-427-2037

MONEY POWER For Families, ISBN 1-56414-049-0, $6.95

To order by mail, please include price as noted above, $2.50 handling per order, plus $1.00 for each book ordered. Send to: Career Press, 180 Fifth Ave., PO Box 34, Hawthorne, NJ 07507. Or call Toll-Free 1-800-CAREER-1 to order using your VISA or Mastercard or for information on all books available from The Career Press.

IMPORTANT: While much careful thought and depth of research have been devoted to the writing of this book, all content is to be viewed as general information only and should not be construed as actual legal, accounting or financial advice of a personal nature.

The ideas, suggestions and general concepts are subject to federal, state and local laws and statutes. The ever-changing economic, political and international environment may well demand reinterpretation of some or all of the concepts presented herein.

The reader is urged to consult competent legal, accounting and tax advisors regarding all legal and personal financial decisions. This book is not meant to be utilized as a substitute for their advice.

Library of Congress Cataloging-in-Publication Data

McAleese, Tama
     Money power for families / by Tama McAleese.
          p.   cm.
     Includes index.
     ISBN 1-56414-049-0
     1. Finance, Personal.   I. Title.
HG179.M3738   1992
332.024--dc20   **92-42043**
                                                           CIP

MONEY POWER
For Families

Introduction

What Your Kids
Mean To You

In this past election year, we heard a lot of rhetoric about "family values." Surely a book about family finances is one place that the discussion should continue.

While most of this book is devoted to the types of numerical "values" that make up the pluses and minuses of a family budget, families will have a hard time deciding what to spend and what *not* spend their money on unless they have managed to forge some agreement about a set of *moral* or *cultural* values. So before we spend nine chapters discussing nothing but dollars and cents, I'm going to take a little time—this introduction—to discuss values.

Raising children has its times of frustration as well as its moments of glory. By the time their children enter kindergarten, parents have made significant progress. Their pre-schooler no longer uses the cereal bowl as a hat substitute, and the diapers are gone. But the teenage (alias "Frankenstein") years can produce tribulations that would have tried the patience of Job. No parent is immune to the ups and downs of adolescence, the key years in which family values may help ensure that this creature becomes an adult you may not only love, but actually like.

Parents get bad news more often than good messages once the Frankenstein years emerge. Like the father of a teenage boy who awoke from an afternoon nap to hear the most dreaded of all questions: "Dad, do you want the good news or the bad news?" His father already had a long list of problems he was trying to forget. "I hear enough bad news," he answered. "Tell me something I can feel good about for a change."

His son answered cheerfully, "You know the airbags on your new car? Well, they work just fine."

I am proud that my children have grown into responsible adults who are contributing something to the world and have learned the meaning of the four-letter word W-O-R-K. They know how to analyze, set and reach goals, and they care about others. A great deal of the credit for the close relationship I share with my children is theirs —they were patient with me. Together we kept the lines of communication open.

Your most important job as a parent is to provide a value structure that is loving, consistent and firm. Sometimes you really do need to "just say no." You may also be a friend and a buddy to your children. But, first and foremost, you must remain a parent in their eyes. If you don't earn their respect, you will never have their love.

You should attempt to understand their culture as much as possible and pretend you are a part of it. This communicates to your teenager the subtle message that you are "cool."

Parents are generally *not* "cool." Everyone *else's* parents are cool. Everyone *else's* parents let their kids stay out late on school nights, go to rock concerts and miss school when their homework is not done. Everyone *else's* parents leave the house when their teenagers throw a party.

Everyone *else's* parents don't show up at parent-teacher conferences, read private notes from boys, look through their drawers when they're not home or "drop in" at their parties. Everyone *else's* parents trust their kids. (And if you believe that monstrous fantasy, I have a bridge I want to sell you.)

You, on the other hand, are not sensitive or loving, don't listen to them when they talk to you, couldn't pos-sibly understand, and, in general, have the sensitivity of soap.

Since you are not perceived as being "cool," you should attempt to change your image. Of course, you are not going to allow your teenager to do all those horrible things listed above. You are just going to present the same illusion of being "cool" that everyone else's parents seem to have mastered. Try the following behavior adaptations:

1. Look your child in the eye as he or she ram-bles on incessantly about the latest disaster in his or her life. As you do this, you can be making mental lists of groceries, chauf-feuring schedules and new recipes to make ground beef look like other things. Throw in some comforting noises such as "...hmmm..." or ...ah..." every few seconds.

    Don't make the common mistake of believing your child actually wants some ad-vice or direction here. He or she just wants to drag someone else into the latest soap opera crisis that highlights adolescence. *Do not* offer any actual counseling or solid advice. If you err here, you will be labeled as a nag, a lec-turer, a drag and unable to cope with a world that is obviously light years away from the cave you were raised in.

2. Keep communications open at all times by discussing any subject they bring up—sex,
drugs, the Simpsons, whatever—especially at
the dinner table, even when guests are present. Never, *never*, **never** mutter, "When I
was your age..." In their minds, this conjures
up a primitive era before CDs, Game Boy and
rap, and immediately destroys any budding
rapport you may have begun to build.

3. Learn that comforting phrase, "This too shall
pass," and repeat it whenever you think you're
losing your sanity. You have neither the time
nor the financial resources for expensive psy-
chological evaluation or long-term therapy at
this point. All financial resources must go
into that college fund.

4. Identify with your child's many phases and
react positively. If your son wants an earring,
respond with an approving comment like,
"Great! Now we can shop and pick out our
jewelry together."

Develop a mental attitude that keeps the important
adolescent times in mind (and in context). A parent may
have greater financial burdens, anxieties and responsibilities, but the joys, the memories and the rainbows you
will share with your kids are some of the most valuable
times of your life.

I wouldn't trade the good times for anything.

Thank goodness nature invented selective amnesia to
erase the "other times!"

If God had wanted kids to be tidy, courteous, continu-
ously thoughtful and never clumsy, He wouldn't have
invented Elmer's glue.

Chapter 1

Step One : Develop A Family Financial Plan

Every family needs a spending and savings plan to set financial goals and maintain a commitment to the most important priorities. A financial plan will also provide reliable data to monitor your progress along the road to your financial success. Where you are now is not nearly as important as the direction in which you are moving.

Arrange a system for handling money.

What are *your* goals?

The first step is for you and your spouse to sit down and determine your financial goals. Do you want to buy a home, or are you content to rent? Will you need a new car soon? Do your children plan to go to college? Will they have the grades and desire to go to the best schools? How much money do you want to donate every year? At what age do you want to retire? When do you realistically think that you can do so comfortably?

Down to the nitty gritty

Once you have established this "big picture," it's time to zero in on the details and establish a monthly budget.

Fill out the monthly cash flow statement on pp. 26 & 27. When completed, post it the refrigerator so that everyone knows the plan under which the family is operating. Underline in a different color ink items that you can cut back on—e.g., insurance premiums, utilities, entertainment, vacations, clothing, etc.

You may have to go through some long family meetings to arrive at a budget that everyone can live with. For example, your kids might be allotted entertainment funds by submitting the costs beforehand. Or, since we live in a democratic nation, you might have them submit these expenses to a family referendum. In that way, the kids would be agreeing to the plan that would determine how much money they could spend.

If all family members understand the total financial picture, they will tend to work harder and display greater tolerance and patience when limited funds thwart their financial desires. Your plan will stand a better chance of success if all major purchases are discussed and mutually agreed upon.

Remember: You must not protect your children from financial realities. This is their only chance to learn valuable money management skills. Otherwise, when they are on their own, they may become walking targets for those who will seduce them to live today and pay it back tomorrow...and tomorrow... and tomorrow.

Some guidelines, of course, must be set by parent edict (otherwise known as "laying down the law"). If your three kids want a Nintendo game and you need two new tires for the car , the majority should not rule. But there are lots of opportunities for discretionary spending that children *can* participate in.

Keep in mind that money can become a source of power over another family member, such as a spouse or teenager. People learn better from positive feedback than from denial, punishment or fear. Financial threats will not achieve long-term family unity and cooperation. Every family member's cheerful help is vital to overall progress.

Once these spending agreements are set, it's time to plan ahead for the entire year. Think about all of the things that will come up—doctor and dentist bills, winter clothes, back-to-school expenses, car repairs, holiday spending, vacations. Divide the anticipated annual expenditures for each of these items by 12 and insert those numbers into your monthly expenses section on the budget. Every month, you should have that money available *even if you don't spend it in that month.*

Putting money aside every month will assure that surprises don't prompt you to throw the budget out with the bath water.

This exercise produces an additional benefit: It gives everyone in the family a long-term perspective that will help them look forward to events with delight rather than anxiety. They will have the assurance that their future needs are being planned for.

Pay yourself first

The most important thing I urge you to do is to rearrange your budget so that savings equal to 10% of your net income come out *first.* This is a "payment" to yourself and your family, rather than to a mortgage banker, utility or credit card company.

This money can be directed toward a variety of goals, such as the emergency or rainy day fund, college fund, a pension plan at work or an IRA account. If you can't manage the whole 10% right now, save as much as you can on a regular basis and increase your contribution as you earn more money or pay off current debts.

Remember those items that you underlined in red on the budget—the expenses that could be reduced? Get the whole family involved so that you can make that 10% payment to your family every month. Don't worry, it won't hurt the kids to be involved in these efforts.

Too many parents keep the family finances a close secret. Giving your kids the straight scoop and making them responsible for sticking to a budget will undoubtedly be beneficial. If your children believe they are a vital part of the family team, they can be proud of their contribution to the family financial plan.

There are many tasks that children can successfully achieve. Turning off the lights, using less soap, toilet paper, toothpaste or laundry detergent, and reducing long-distance phone calls are examples. Engaging in baby-sitting or newspaper delivery will allow them to earn their own spending money and thus contribute to family savings or create their own spending money. Children are very imaginative. By showing them the areas where savings can be achieved, you will elicit their creative methods for reducing expenses.

Enlist the kids' help in the hunt for low-cost or free family entertainment activities such as county park events, community festivals, local sporting events, biking, museum and wildlife tours and family picnics. This will, in addition to cutting living expenses, strengthen family ties and encourage communication.

If at first...

If you fail to stick to your budget, don't throw up your hands. Find out why it failed and make adjustments. Then try again.

Review your plan once a month. Hold family counsels on it. Let everyone know where it has been successful and where it has broken down. Make each family member responsible for some part of the plan's success.

Do *not* attach blame. There is probably enough to go around. Instead, praise positive steps. If your son has stopped leaving your tools in the rain to rust, this is a step forward. If your daughter has taken 3 fewer showers per day, greatly reducing your water bill, applaud her efforts.

There must be rewards for success. Set aside a small amount of money as a family reward for entertainment or an outing. Going to Mouseland is *not* an eight-year-old's birthright. It is a privilege and a huge expenditure. It and similar large financial goals should be achieved through family teamwork.

Significant progress might take time. Look for small but obvious signs of financial improvement and broadcast this good news to the entire family. Children can check monthly utility bills to see how their efforts reduced costs. Phone bills are easy to monitor and compare with last month's long distance charges. Rewarding children for *not* spending is just as important as encouraging their wise use of spending.

Avoiding the most common money mistakes

Most families typically make mistakes with their money that are easy to avoid if you develop a spending plan similar to that which we've outlined here:

1. *They depend on others for their financial futures,* like the government (Social Security) and their company (pension). They turn over basic investment decisions to strangers and give up managing their own assets. Financial institutions that want to manage your assets are middlemen to be avoided whenever possible.

2. *They don't understand the rules of the Money Game,* like how compound interest and time affect money and how inflation reduces its power over time.

3. *They get caught in "loanership" positions.* Living on credit is our country's number one financial problem. It is a clever industry that can teach consumers to pay more and more each day for something that becomes worth less and less.

4. *They don't understand the theory of decreasing responsibility* in terms of risk management needs. In most cases, you should protect your *liabilities*, not your assets. Most people buy the wrong types of insurance, pay too much for it, and still wind up poorly insured.

5. *They purchase insurance products for the wrong reasons,* without understanding their contracts, and put their savings at risk inside these institutions.

6. *They are willing to believe unrealistic expectations of return* for products that they do *not* really understand.

7. *They pay themselves last.* They procrastinate when it comes to saving money for their futures.

8. *They overpay on taxes* and don't understand the impact of tax brackets and tax-sheltered vehicles such as IRA accounts, SEPs and KEOGHs. They do, however, purchase too many investment products purely for tax purposes, allowing the tax tail to wag the investment dog.

9. *They utilize outmoded investment vehicles* and give up the flexibility to move as time changes.

✗ The last generation bought a home, put some money in the bank and sent the rest of their savings to the insurance industry. None of those are appropriate long-term investment vehicles.

10. *They listen to their parents.* Families pass on traditions that didn't work for them and won't work for you. Your home is the largest but the lousiest investment you can make. View it as a nest; put your investment assets in other vehicles.

11. *They don't watch after their own money.* Without a financial education, they compromise liquidity, flexibility of investment goals and higher rates of return for products that sound good but have time-loss factors, low real rates of return and high surrender costs if you decide to leave.

12. *Most folks set no financial goals* or the means to reach them. Dreams do not just happen; they are planned for and adjusted over time.

Keeping fiscally fit

Today's emphasis on physical fitness is a positive sign that consumers are taking charge of their health over the long-term. However, to be able to enjoy those extra years of healthy living, you must also be *fiscally* fit.

- Complete a written financial plan, either prepared by yourself or by a professional financial planner, to identify short-term and long-term goals and the means to achieve them.
- Compile a budget detailing where you are now and in which primary direction those paycheck dollars are flowing. Research areas where you

can conserve costs or find better value for dollars spent.

- Develop an emergency fund consisting of three to six months of your take-home pay. If this is impossible, attempt to have at least two months' reserve. This should be put into a liquid investment with little risk to principal.

- Start funding college early with as little as $25 or $50 per month in a good mutual fund. Initiate a systematic monthly investment plan through payroll deduction, your checking account or a credit union. This is long-term money that must outpace inflation, so provide for more than just fixed-income vehicles. Achieve some growth.

- Look for tax advantages that will enhance your portfolio *without* reducing or limiting your primary objectives: (1) the purpose for the investment, and (2) the best investment vehicle considering the time your money has to work. Don't purchase tax-advantaged investments just to beat the IRS.

- If you are receiving a large IRS refund, increase monthly deductions and put that extra money to work for you through automatic savings plans that remove the savings before you see them. That way, you won't spend them.

- Start *now* on your retirement funding, even if you are young. It takes less seed money to create that large pot over time than if you wait until you are older.

- As you income increases, don't increase your lifestyle. Instead, stash those dollars for future financial goals. Live *beneath* your means.

- It's not what you earn on your investments that counts; it's what you can keep *after* inflation. Keep track of the *real* inflation rate, and monitor your portfolio to outpace it.
- Understand what your company health, death and retirement benefits are. Consider these basic coverage only. You may need additional protection.
- Create an estate plan and have a durable power ↵ *HOWE* of attorney drawn up. This gives someone else (who you name) the ability to manage your financial affairs in case you become disabled. Send for a living will kit (if appropriate in your state) to make medical decisions clear if you can't.
- Create a will to control disbursement of your assets, the guardianship of your children and the trustee of their assets. Modify your estate plan each time your health, personal or financial life changes significantly.
- Calculate long-term college tuition needs and retirement fund needs by using the Rule of 72, which will give you a ballpark figure of how you are doing toward accumulating those needed funds at the appropriate time.
- Pay off your consumer credit card debt as quickly as possible while still contributing to your emergency fund. A budget will help determine how much extra you have for that challenge.

When you have completed the above steps, you will be in great fiscal shape. Until then, keep making slow but steady progress to put yourself in charge of your financial life and guarantee a successful financial future.

HOW TO SUCCESSFULLY COMPLETE YOUR FINANCIAL PLAN

1. Start today.

2. Include at least your spouse in your discussions.

3. Fill out the basic goals and objectives worksheet.

4. Don't attach blame—there is probably enough for everyone to share.

5. Fill out *completely* the monthly cash flow statement.

6. Group items in the following categories: 1) savings & investments; 2) home mortgage or rental expenses; 3) consumer debt; and 4) disposable income expenses.

7. Star those areas that can be reduced (e.g., insurance premiums, utilities, entertainment, vacations, consumer spending, etc.).

 8. Compare net *(not gross)* take-home pay to outgoing monthly expenses.

9. Take necessary steps to balance the budget. Someone may need to bring home extra income for a time.

10. Put your budget on the refrigerator where it can be seen and followed.

HOW TO SUCCESSFULLY
COMPLETE YOUR FINANCIAL PLAN

11. Immediately develop a back-up emergency fund.

12. Start a monthly systematic savings plan.

13. Negotiate occasional monetary rewards to reduce financial stress.

14. If you suffer temporary budget overflows, start again as soon as possible.

15. Work on debt management at the same time that you develop an emergency fund.

16. Don't become too zealous in paying off consumer debt at the expense of developing a savings plan.

17. Even a small amount each month should be saved. As income and other financial burdens improve, increase savings.

18. Cut your consumer debt; if necessary, cut the credit cards.

19. Turn your finances around patiently. Look for signs of progress.

GOALS, OBJECTIVES & ATTITUDES WORKSHEET

Date: _____

List all your objectives under the following major categories—the more specific the better.

Retirement: _____

_____

_____

_____

_____

_____

_____

_____

Estate Planning: _____

_____

_____

_____

_____

_____

_____

_____

Educational: _____

_____

_____

_____

_____

_____

_____

Income (Is additional current income needed?):

_____

_____

_____

_____

_____

Other: _____

_____

_____

_____

_____

_____

ATTITUDE CHECK

1. Rank the preceding objectives in order of priority.

2. Target overall after-tax return per year: _____
   (If all bank deposits, figure 3.5%; if some growth vehicles, figure 7.2%.)

3. Expected inflation rate: ____ (Expect an average of 6% per year.)

4. Would you alter your current lifestyle to attain your objectives? YES

5. How active do you want to be in managing your investments? (Note: Individual stocks, bonds, and other issues require active management.)
   ❑ Very active ❑ Somewhat active
   ❑ Not very active ❑ Inactive

6. Define short-term objectives (less than 3 years):

PAY-OFF ALL CREDIT CARDS

COMPLETE 4 MO EMERGENCY FUND (12,5)

(12,488)

7. Define long-term objectives (more than 3 years):

ELIMINATE MORTGAGE PAYMNT (7 YRS)

PAY FOR COLLEGE EDUCATIONS (2)

SAVE FOR RETIREMENT

8. How much risk can you (or are you willing to) tolerate?

☐ A lot ☐ A fair amount ☐ Not a little, not a lot
☑ A little ☐ As little as possible

9. Are there areas you would *not* consider for financial objectives? ☐ Yes ☑ No

If so, what? _____

10. Please rank the following in order of their importance to you:

____2____ 1) Financial provisions for family/spouse (in case of death)

____4____ 2) Retirement income needs for yourself/spouse

____1____ 3) Educational plans

____3____ 4) Special plans or objectives

HOW TO SUCCESSFULLY DEVELOP A WORKING MONTHLY BUDGET

1. Calculate monthly expenses for all listed categories on the Cash Flow Statement.

2. Estimate variable outflows such as utilities, clothing and car and home maintenance.

3. Divide occasional bills such as taxes and insurance premiums into monthly payments.

4. Utilize a strategy for accumulating Christmas funds.

5. Examine all categories to reduce outgoing expenses (e.g., auto, homeowner and life insurance, entertainment, miscellaneous).

6. Total all expenses and list in the "Monthly Expenses" space.

7. Calculate all dependable net income. (To translate weekly paychecks into monthly figures, multiply by 4.3.) Try not to include overtime.

8. List all net income in the space "Net Take-Home Pay."

HOW TO SUCCESSFULLY DEVELOP A WORKING MONTHLY BUDGET

9. Pay yourself first.
10. Pay all other bills in order of their priority.
11. Keep remaining money set aside for future payments in an interest-bearing account.
12. Develop an emergency fund.
13. Remember what the word "emergency" means.
14. Compile current assets on the Portfolio Planning Worksheet.
15. Reduce overpayments on federal taxes by increasing deductions.
16. Sign up for an automatic payroll or checking deduction plan to transfer that income for future financial goals.
17. Discuss and negotiate every major capital expenditure.
18. Keep the budget handy and in full view as a reminder and commitment.
19. Stick to your plan—reevaluate it over time.

MONTHLY CASH FLOW STATEMENT

Net Take-Home Pay *3122* _____
Monthly Expenses: *≈ 2950* _____
Fritter Money (Take-Home Pay
Minus Expenses): *≈ 122* _____

Monthly Expense Detail

10% Savings and Investments: _____
   EMERGENCY FUND 100/mo
   Include company pension plans, individual retirement plans (IRAs, KEOGHs, etc.), establishing an
   emergency fund and general investment accounts

22% Housing Costs
   Monthly Mortgage Payment/Rent: *985* _____
   Property Taxes (per month): _____—_____
   Property Insurance(per month): ____—_____
   Home Equity Loan Payments: _____←_____

18% Consumer Debt
   Dept. Store Accounts: _____
   Credit Card Accounts: *≈ 300* _____
   Bank Loans: *234,336 = 570* _____
   Car Payment(s): *234+336 570* _____
   Other Time Payments: _____

50% Other Monthly Expenses
   *Child Support/Alimony: _____
   *Electricity: *⎱ 150/mo* _____
   *Heat: *⎰* _____

                    SUBT. 2105

*Telephone: #7 0/mo _____
*Water: 45/QTR 12/mo _____
*Auto Insurance: 150/mo _____
*Life Insurance: 30/mo _____
*Medical/Dental: 20/mo _____
*Other Insurance: 240/mo _____
*Groceries: 240/mo _____
*Gasoline/Diesel: 172/mo _____
*Car Maintenance: 20/mo _____
*Entertainment: 20/mo _____
*Cable TV: _____
*Clothing: 80/mo _____
*Vacation: _____
*School Tuition: _____
*School Supplies: _____
*Organization Dues: _____
*Subscriptions: 10/mo _____
*Household Items: 20/mo _____
*Miscellaneous: _____
Total: ≈ 844 _____

*This area may have to be slashed to allow for savings and investments and overruns in other areas. If monies used for "other monthly expenses" represent *less* than 50% of total take-home pay, other areas can be expanded —e.g., purchasing a bigger home or increasing the savings and investing portion.

Present Lump Sum Obligations

Mortgage Balance: _____
College Tuition: _____
Other: _____

Personal Portfolio Planning Worksheet

Short-term Financial Objective:_____

Long-term Financial Objective:_____

1. Cash and cash equivalents/short-term money (Checking and savings accounts, credit unions and rainy-day money)

Where Deposited	Objective	$ Value	Rate of Return
_____	_____	_____	_____
_____	_____	_____	_____
_____	_____	_____	_____
_____	_____	_____	_____
_____	_____	_____	_____
_____	_____	_____	_____
_____	_____	_____	_____
_____	_____	_____	_____

2. Securities/long-term money (bank CDs, annuities, mutual funds, stocks, bonds, etc.)

Investment or Security	Interest Rate	$ Value	Maturity Date
_____	_____	_____	_____
_____	_____	_____	_____

_____   _____   _____   _____

_____   _____   _____   _____

_____   _____   _____   _____

_____   _____   _____   _____

_____   _____   _____   _____

_____   _____   _____   _____

_____   _____   _____   _____

_____   _____   _____   _____

_____   _____   _____   _____

3. Regular Investment Programs

Name of Vehicle	Amount Invested	Frequency	Current Yield	Present Value

Chapter 2

Keeping More Of What You Earn

Get-rich-quick schemes all involve ways to *make* money. An important component of my get-rich-*slow* philosophy is to *keep* more of the money that you have already worked so hard to make. Here are some important and simple ways to do that:

1. Cancel brokerage accounts, and manage your own investments to reduce fees. You're not a high-flying financier. Put your money into mutual funds where you will get management services at a low cost and effectively cut out the middleman.

2. Wait to pay bills and make some more interest on the money you have in an interest-bearing checking account.

3. Set up an automatic investment account for retirement.

4. Drop a credit card—preferably the one with the highest annual percentage rate. Then drop the one with the next highest rate until you get rid of most of your plastic. Paying for revolving credit at loan-shark rates is just too expensive.

done ✓

5. Don't prepay low-interest loans. If the interest is low enough, inflation is probably making up for the interest payments.

6. Don't overpay income taxes during the year. If you get a big refund, take more deductions during the year. You should not be Uncle Sam's banker.

7. Increase your current death insurance coverage by the amount of your outstanding mortgage balance—then discontinue lender mortgage insurance. A family with children and a mortgage needs $250,000 or more insurance coverage while the wage earner is young and before significant assets have been accumulated. Buy term insurance for the greatest death benefit, and start a separate investment plan to take care of retirement.

8. Switch regular checking accounts to interest-bearing ones.

9. Review club memberships with annual dues.

10. Seek out the maximum interest on your emergency fund. Check several local lenders' rates on interest-bearing accounts.

11. Defer income and accelerate deductible expenses if the underlying economic purposes for such actions are sound. Don't borrow a dollar to achieve 28 cents in tax-deductible savings, unless it makes good economic sense to do so.

12. Quit smoking, and put the money you would have spent in a special account. Reward yourself for quitting and let the leftover money work hard for you.

13. Liquidate debts with interest charges greater than your investment return would be.

AFTER EMERGENCY FUND

14. Switch personal credit to home equity loans, as long as you're sure you can repay them.

15. Switch to lower-interest credit cards if you are unable to get rid of plastic altogether.

16. Review homeowner's and auto insurance and comparison shop.

17. Consider refinancing your mortgage if current percentage rates justify it.

18. Start an IRA for your working teenagers. They will thank you for it someday.

19. Accelerate deductions—bunch them together every other year.

20. Transfer children's medical expenses to their tax returns if you can itemize the deductions in this manner.

21. Keep deductible IRAs, non-deductible IRAs and IRA rollovers separate.

Chapter 3

Teaching Your Children The Value Of Money

Too many children believe that spending is a fun activity, while saving is the penalty for being born to a middle-class family of financial nerds. Spending becomes rewarding, while saving is looked on with the same general disgust as homework and braces.

Children *should* be taught to look at saving merely as deferred spending—putting off spending right now so the money compounds into a much larger pot to fund greater future spending. A spendthrift child makes an ideal candidate for this concept. If he or she loves spending so much, get him or her to think how great it would feel to spend even *more* in the future because they've saved their money and allowed it to grow over time.

Although personal money management is one of the most important skills kids can learn, it is not taught in most schools. Students can graduate with marvelous money-making skills, yet not have a clue how to *manage* the small fortune they will earn during their working years.

A parent can eliminate a student's naivete before their credit card debt mounts, before the 30-year lifetime indentured mortgage is signed for and before they learn to live beyond their financial means.

Developing a family financial plan at an early age helps them set priorities. It teaches that compromises must be made and spending alternatives weighed. This is a vital training ground for when they make independent decisions regarding finances.

Review the attitude checklist below with your children. It will provide all of you with a starting point for discussing their spending and saving habits.

1. _____ I see money as a means to buy something now.

2. _____ Money burns a hole in my pocket until it is spent.

3. _____ I purchase things, but seldom get long-lasting pleasure.

4. _____ Saving is very important to me.

5. _____ I spend more than I save.

6. _____ I save more than I spend.

7. _____ I have a difficult time saving.

8. _____ I wish I could save more.

9. _____ Spending money makes me happy.

10. _____ Money satisfies my long-term financial goals.

11. _____ $5 is a lot of money to me.

12. _____ $50 is a lot of money to me.

13. _____ If I had $100 ($1,000, $10,000), I would feel rich.

14. _____ I would like to be more responsible financially.

15. _____ If I were given $50 today, I would spend it all.

16. _____ If I were given $100, I would spend it all.
17. _____ I only save to purchase small items.
18. _____ I can save up for larger purchases.
19. _____ I believe even a small amount of money can be powerful.
20. _____ I feel better (worse) when I spend my own money.

When you are alone, read the above list and answer it yourself. A parent's greatest teaching method is by example. If you wonder where your kids are learning poor financial habits, perhaps you now have the answer.

The right start

Developing a working budget is a must, even for a teenager. The budget will reveal a pattern of saving and spending that can be analyzed and improved while your child is still living at home. The goal of managing money well is the satisfaction of every dollar earned, saved and spent.

Help your adolescent learn to examine the following:

1. The total price of the item—not just the down payment;
2. The quality of the product;
3. How long the purchase is made to last;
4. How durable the product or item is;
5. How often the item will be used;
6. How much upkeep or repair will be needed;

7. How necessary the purchase is;
8. The opportunity cost of buying any specific item;
9. Whether they really need this item now;
10. If they can really afford this item now.

Opportunity knocks

Opportunity cost is the key to wise personal money management and efficient spending habits. If your child has $50 and spends it entirely on a movie and entertainment for friends, the *opportunity cost* is all the other things he or she could have done with the $50 right now *and* all the lost opportunities to use that same $50 in the future.

Opportunity cost is not a moral issue. It is an awareness that decisions must be made, financial resources are limited and priorities must be set before financial resources are allocated. Too many teenagers and adults are living examples of the old saying: "Money talks, I'll not deny. I heard it once—it said 'Good-bye.'"

What about an allowance?

My children never received an allowance simply because they were born into our family. Why should they? I did all the work: I got pregnant, I got morning sickness, I got fat. Then I went into labor, a state of profound "discomfort." (Male obstretricians always use that word. If they told women how much pain was really in store, we would find a way to make our husbands bear children.) Then it took the next 25 years to raise and educate them.

Many parents choose to give their children incentive allowances for chores performed around the house. Just be sure this scheme doesn't bite you back. A child can quickly learn that he or she should be paid for everything, and self-interest might become the motive for pitching in.

A family team works together without thought of reimbursement. If your teenager suddenly threatens to strike for more money while your garbage smells up the kitchen, you have created a monster.

If you do give your children some money of their own, you shouldn't punish them by withholding allowances or reneging on entertainment and activity funds. Supervised money management is your child's only financial training ground for the future.

Value lessons come automatically with their use—or misuse—of money. When the allowance is spent and your children come to you for additional funds, sympathize with their financial plight, but provide no financial disaster aid. When they receive their next allowance, encourage them to manage it a little better.

Kids spend 24 hours a day plotting against their parents, while parents seldom huddle together to develop defensive strategies. One clothes-shopping trip with a teenager will convince you that you are an amateur up against a professional. Instead of defending your depleted checking account balance in front of store clerks who have mistaken you for Cinderella's cheap stepmother, send your teenagers shopping *without* you.

Give them the amount you have budgeted for their clothing allowance (cash, not credit cards), and let them make the final choices. When the money is gone, they will come home. The trick here is that once the money has been spent, *there is no more* until your next regularly scheduled underwear and coat buying day.

You will be amazed at the transformation.

Your children will become lean, mean financial fighting machines when they believe it is *their* money being spent.

If this first experiment fails and you fear for the flu season because the entire clothing allowance bought one New Year's Eve satin dress, don't wimp out and send more money to the front lines. *Last* winter's old coat will be a suitable teacher. The next time you send your kids shopping, they will spend their (your) money much more wisely.

Checking in

Many years ago I heard rumors that someday real money would be taken away and in its place we would be given only funny money. At the time it seemed like some cult philosophy. But it has come true.

I think one reason the younger generation is so unaware of the value of money is that they rarely spend *real* greenbacks. Instead, they write numbers on pink bunnies, yellow ducks and purple mountain's majesty—called checks.

Or they give retailers a piece of Mom or Dad's plastic, then get the plastic back with some merchandise as well, never to see a bill!

A checking account or a credit card must not allow your kids to feel richer than they really are. It must not lead them to believe they can use tomorrow's income to pay for today's purchases. Wants and needs are two different things. Help them separate one from the other.

Teach your children well

A portion of all your children's earned income and all allowance money should be directed to a savings account, a piggy bank or some other method to "pay themselves first." They need to understand the wonderful power of compound interest and the insidious evils of inflation.

Every child needs an emergency fund or rainy day account so they will not turn to short-term credit, a quick fix for financial problems.

Good spending and saving habits will last your children a lifetime. Sharing with them information on the family's financial goals, giving them a say in the budgeting process and not allowing them to spend, spend, spend will make them grateful to you forever.

Sure, it will bring about some heated arguments, but it's better than having them come back home some day with their spouses and kids because they spent themselves into the poorhouse!

Chapter 4

Giving Credit Where It Is Due

Shopping for borrowed money is similar to shopping for curtains, a new car or any other purchase. Different outlets have different prices, some companies have periodic sales and the burden is on the buyer to ferret out and separate the good deals from the bad.

The better plastic

Credit cards are individual agreements set up by banking institutions, credit unions and other entities. Since the competition in this market is getting fiercer, the terms of the agreements offered by various institutions will vary significantly.

Use the following questions to comparison shop and find the type of credit card right for your purposes:

1. What is the annual fee? Can it go up in the future?

2. What is the annual percentage rate? Is it fixed or variable?

3. What is the grace period before interest starts? (Some low interest-rate cards have no grace period at all—you are

charged interest from the moment you make the purchase.) How is interest charged?

4. Is there a charge for late payments? How much?

5. Are there transaction fees for purchases?

6. What is the annual percentage rate for cash advances? Is it higher than the interest charged for purchases?

7. Is the minimum monthly payment lower than the previous month's interest charge?

8. When does interest start after I request a cash advance?

9. Is there a user fee or transaction fee for each cash advance?

10. How much does the lender charge for over-the-limit purchases?

11. Are there agreements in the fine print?

12. Have you read every word in the application?

13. Have you understood every word you've read?

14. Can you afford another credit card right now?

15. Will you save interest (not gain lower payments on a larger loan) by switching existing debt to a new credit card?

16. Does your budget show enough income to pay for your new purchases?

17. How much credit do you absolutely need?
18. What credit limit can you afford?
19. How will this new financial obligation affect your existing debt level?
20. Will this new credit limit encourage you to feel richer than you really are?
21. Do you understand that credit cards are for emergencies and convenience only and *not* methods of buying more than you can afford?

Your personal credit crunch

As the last few questions suggest, I am not a big fan of revolving debt. So many American families are facing a "credit card crunch" that they need budgetary intensive care to alleviate the burden of too much debt.

Is your family in a credit card crunch? Here are some of the warning signs:

- You don't know how much total debt you owe (just the size of the payments), and you're afraid to add it all up. Perhaps you even hide monthly statements from your family;

- You pay only minimum monthly payments—or less—each month;

- You have reached your credit limits on some cards and are more actively borrowing with others to make up the cash difference;

- You borrow for purchases you used to buy with cash;

- The portion of your income used to pay debts is rising, and you no longer contribute to a savings or investment account. You have little or no emergency fund savings;

- You are often late paying some of your bills, and you juggle the budget to keep up. This month's credit balances are even larger than they were *last* month;

- You have borrowed money to pay for regular household expenses such as rent, food, clothing, gas or insurance. You borrowed more money to pay off an overdue debt or have just consolidated loans. Now you're applying for additional credit cards to borrow even *more* money;

- You are currently drawing from savings to pay regular bills and have little or no rainy day money left—you don't have enough savings for at least three months' living expenses if you are laid off, disabled or become ill;

- Your liquid assets (savings) total less than your short-term debt, and you often use a cash advance from one credit card to make payments on others. You are paying regular bills with money earmarked for other obligations. More than 18% of your after-tax income goes toward consumer installment debt;

- Creditors are sending overdue notices. You postdate checks so payments won't bounce, then hurry to the bank on payday

to cover checks already written. Checks
are bouncing on a more frequent basis;

• Life without credit seems unthinkable.

Emergency room prescription

My prescription is that you pay down your consumer
debt slowly but surely. I can promise you a risk-free,
guaranteed double-digit rate of return—anywhere from
18% to 23%—if you will simply pay off your credit card
balances.

Sit down tonight (with the rest of your family, if possible) and make a new commitment to financial freedom.
First, list all your credit cards, the total balances due,
their annual percentage rates and the minimum monthly payments. (Use the form on p. 46.)

Total up your budget and subtract all dependable
monthly take-home income. The remaining money is the
"fat" left over, dollars that are slipping away without
value. Recapture their value by dividing them in two.
Deposit one-half into an emergency fund to pay yourself
first; direct the other half to the card with the highest
interest rate.

The size of the balance does not matter. It is the cost
for the borrowed money (the interest rate) that really
counts. Be careful: Annual percentage rates are deceptive
because they lead you to believe that the interest is not
compounded, while the monthly interest is compounded
each and every month throughout the year on an unpaid
credit balance. You will pay almost 2% more interest per
year than the stated interest rate if you pay your credit
card debts over long installments.

Do not become so zealous with paying off debt that you
forget to build your emergency fund. If you should find

yourself short of cash, you will just borrow again, reversing and progress and putting yourself further into the debt hole. You didn't get into this mess overnight. Dig yourself out slowly and systematically.

And now that you've fully realized you're in a hole, for goodness sakes, stop digging! Whatever happens, don't borrow any more money until your current debt is gone.

When you have paid off the highest annual percentage rate (APR) card, start on another. In the meantime, pay monthly minimums only on all the others, and keep building your rainy day money fund.

Once you are debt-free, maintain your budget and direct those previous credit card payments to the emergency fund or long-term savings plan.

CREDIT CARD COMPARISON SHEET

Issuer	Amount Owed	APR	Annual Fee	Minimum Payment

Chapter 5

Your Home: Maybe Not Your *Best* Investment

This chapter flies in the face of one of the most pervasive myths that is part and parcel of the American Dream. Many people sink their life savings into homes, thinking that they are risk-free investments and effective inflation fighters. The downturn in housing prices in most areas of the country over the last two years or more has proved otherwise.

Your home is the *largest* investment you will make. It is perhaps the *lousiest*. But generally it won't be one of the top ten *best* investments you'll ever made.

The disadvantages are many

Let's consider the four key disadvantages of home ownership.

1. *It is not a liquid investment.* If you needed $20,000, could you sell your kitchen overnight to get it? Of course not. But you could write a check from a mutual fund or sell a CD within a matter of minutes.

2. *You are buying your castle with expensive borrowed money.* Over the life of a 30-year

conventional mortgage, you will be giving the bank nearly three times the amount that you borrowed. That is, if you purchased a $100,000 home today (are there many of those out there these days?), you would have to sell it for $300,000 in 30 years just to recapture the money you've paid to the lender.

3. *There are many other costs involved*—insurance, real estate taxes, assessments, improvements, maintenance, closing costs at purchase and selling time—all of which also come right out of your pocket.

4. *Inflation might work against you.* While home prices usually rise with the rate of inflation, that is not always the case. Recently we've seen a depreciation of home prices in many parts of the country, while inflation has continued to lope along at 5% or so.

But I have to live somewhere, don't I?

For years, Americans have believed that they should buy "all the house" they could afford, mortgaging themselves up to the hilt, because, after all, they would be making the best investment possible.

Folks have invested in residential real estate at the expense of their emergency funds, their IRA contributions, company pension plans, even their college savings. Nothing speaks louder against this argument than numbers. So, let's do some basic housing math.

Assume a couple purchased a house for $25,000 20 years ago and sold it today for $75,000. If we eliminate the costs associated with home upkeep and improving it so they could command that selling price, real estate taxes, insurance, closing costs and commissions for the real estate agents, it would appear that the couple made a fat profit of 200% over 20 years.

However, it took our couple 20 years to make that profit. Applying some basic math, we find that they made a profit of 5.647% on their initial investment. Meanwhile, they could have been receiving 8% to 9% per year on a variety of other investments that wouldn't have needed painting, landscaping or gutter cleaning. What's more, those other investments would have been liquid.

In addition, since they didn't have $25,000 to invest 20 years ago, they made a 10% down payment of $2,500 and borrowed the rest at 9% interest.

When they purchased the house, a $1,750 real estate commission had been built into the sales price. They also had to pay $2,000 for closing costs and points on their mortgage. The mortgage they signed called for monthly payments of $202.44 for the duration of the mortgage. In addition, they had to fork over $600 per year in property taxes, $200 per year for insurance and $500 per year, on average, for basic upkeep. Over the life of the mortgage, these outlays totaled $26,000.

And when our friends sold their home sweet home, they incurred another real estate commission and additional lawyer's fees totaling $7,000.

Add it all up—the down payment, insurance, property taxes, minimal upkeep, closing costs, real estate commissions and the cost of the money they had to borrow for 20 years—and we find that the couple paid $87,835 for their investment. And they received $75,000.

That means they actually *lost* $12,835 on what many people say is the best investment they could make.

I know what you're thinking: *I'm dead wrong.* I have not even considered the tax advantages of owning a home.

Yes, I did leave the tax advantages out of the equation, but I also left out a lot of other things. For example, I assumed that property taxes would not increase over the 20-year span of the investment. In addition, our friends' insurance didn't increase. And, miraculously, they did not need any major repairs during 20 years of home-ownership: The boiler never quit in the middle of February, the exterior paint stayed pristine, their lawn just grew every year without seeding and fertilizing, and they never had any major damage to their pipes or electrical system. (Our friends are just about the luckiest people on the planet!) And I neglected to include the effects of inflation on their investment.

But let's look at their attractive tax write-off in the best possible light. Assume that every red cent—all $87,835 that they paid out during the 20 years they owned their home—could be written off their taxes (which is unrealistic). Let's also assume that he was a doctor, she was a lawyer and they were in the 50% tax bracket during all of their years under that roof (even though there is no longer any such thing as a 50% tax bracket). That would mean that they achieved tax savings of $43,917.50, one-half of the total amount of money that the investment cost them. There. That means our couple *made* $31,082.50 on their investment.

The numbers really don't lie

Ah, there are the profits, you're saying. Those home-owners were able to write off their costs for living under a roof, while renters are merely giving that money away every month without the value of tax write-offs and investment in a saleable asset.

Rather than argue this point, let's go back to the numbers. Assume that our couple simply could not afford that

$25,000 house 20 years ago, so they decided to invest their savings at a modest 8% per year. And let's further assume that they could have rented a nice abode for the monthly equivalent of their mortgage payment.

So they placed their $2,500 down payment and the closing costs and commissions ($3,750) they were supposed to pay at the very beginning and invested that total ($6,250) for 20 years, reinvesting the interest earned along the way.

On January 1 every year since, they took the $1,300 they would have paid over to some municipality in taxes, and the money they would have spent on insurance, maintenance and other home ownership costs and invested that as well (this is one smart couple!).

And, at the end of those 20 years, they placed the $7,000 they would have had to fork over for commissions and lawyer fees for selling the house in a non-interest-bearing checking account.

The happy result: Thanks to the wonderful magic of compound interest, they would have $100,381 at the end of 20 years, *more than three times* the amount they would have earned by owning a place to live.

Believe it or not—and you should; these numbers do not lie—this is a true comparison.

But what about pride of ownership?

That's one thing that you can't itemize in a column of numbers. But that illusion of wealth may be an awfully expensive source of pride. No matter how nice you think the kitchens and bathrooms are, no matter how people "ooh" and "ah" when they see "what you've done with the place," buy the home you *need*, not the biggest and best that someone else tells you you can afford. Then *invest the rest of your precious dollars somewhere else*.

I am not advocating that you live in an appliance carton for the next 20 years. I'm simply advising you to choose a home you can afford instead of one that may put your college and retirement savings at risk.

Buying the right home

How much should you spend on a home so that you can give your family a nice place to live in a good neighborhood with white picket fences and good schools?

The first thing to do is look at the monthly line for take-home pay in your budget, multiply it by 22%, and consider that the *maximum* housing payment (which includes mortgage, real estate taxes and homeowner's insurance) you can afford. Then, go to your lender to pre-qualify for a 15- or 20-year loan (only serious criminals should get 30-year sentences).

Determine the type of loan that's best for you—fixed-rate or adjustable. The latter offers attractively low initial rates, but can increase substantially if you live in your home for a number of years. Generally speaking, it's best to get a fixed-interest mortgage.

Not sure about this? Then have the lender print out several scenarios so you can see the effects rising interest rates might have on your family's bottom line. Ask about the cap (maximum payment) that the adjustable rate mortgage (ARM) can climb to.

A-hunting we will go

Once you've qualified for the loan, it's time to go shopping. I cannot stress how important it is to show up as a *pre*-qualified buyer. Walking into must-sell situations (due to bankruptcy, divorce, relocation, death, etc.), you will have additional leverage if the owner knows you are someone who can take the house off his or her hands quickly, without the time and uncertainty involved in the mortgage-approval process.

But before you go shopping, you must be prepared to defend your pocketbook from the real estate industry, which may encourage you to purchase "too much house." Whatever their arguments, you must stoicly resist, insisting that you have only $_____ per month to spend for your mortgage, taxes and insurance (based on your 22% budget figure).

Then, keep in mind the three major rules of purchasing real estate: 1) location; 2) location; and 3) location. Look for one of the least expensive homes in the best neighborhood you can afford.

Once you've found a home that your family likes, walk around the neighborhood *without* the real estate agent at your elbow. Talk to the neighbors about how many kids are in the neighborhood, what they think of the schools. Then contact the county and municipal planning agencies to find out if there are any major building projects planned for the area that might adversely affect real estate values.

Be sure to insist that engineering, electrical and termite inspections are performed before you buy the house. You definitely want to be fully informed and make sure that the seller takes care of most of the house's problems *before* you pay for it.

Bargain hunting

Remember that bidding and counterbidding are part of the house-buying game. You are no more expected to pay the list price for a house than you are to pay the sticker price for a new car. Don't be afraid of putting in a low bid. Do you care if you hurt the owner's feelings?

Bank or sheriff's sales and auctions could represent good deal-making opportunities. But be careful about taking part in any auction if you haven't had an adequate opportunity to inspect your potential purchase.

The most expensive financial blunder you can be talked into by mortgage lenders and the real estate industry is purchasing a home you really can't afford to impress a lot of acquaintances you don't really like.

When these institutions assure you that your dream house is affordable and you "owe it to yourself" now, remind yourself of the other goals you may be sacrificing by tackling such a treacherous pile of debt.

Chapter 6

The Hassle
Of The Tassel

When your child finally walks down the aisle at college graduation, you will be very proud. You might even temporarily forget all the sacrifices you have made up to that day. Unfortunately, if you are a middle income parent, the higher education years will be your biggest test yet in the college of financial knowledge.

If your children are still young, you have the magic ingredient to meet this final challenge: time. The most valuable gift you can give your new baby is a monthly investment plan of $25 or $50 in a high-quality mutual fund.

The current four-year cost of a public university is approximately $32,500, in return for which you would rightly expect them to name a gymnasium or art wing after you. However, if you are planning a new addition to your family, you will need between $125,000 and $150,000 18 years from now to fund the same quality education. The jump is due to inflation, that pesky enemy that keeps popping up and forcing us to invest our long-term assets for some growth of principal.

The further away your college goal, the more money you will ultimately spend. But as long as your college fund is regularly outpacing the higher costs of education, your goals become more reachable. You must choose inflation-fighting investment vehicles that will race against the long-term erosion of your purchasing power.

Many parents choose the wrong type of investment vehicles and wind up on the steps of Ivy University short of needed funds. By investing in fixed-income investments like zero coupon bonds, bank deposits, savings bonds, insurance policies or annuities, or U.S. Government notes, they eliminate the potential for growth that is imperative to stay ahead of inflation.

You will never catch up with college tuition increasing at a steady 8% to 12% per year with a 6% U.S. Government Series EE bond, even if it comes with tax-free advantages under certain circumstances. You need greater inflation-fighting power.

There are some basic mistakes parents make in planning for the higher education of their children:

1. Waiting too long to start saving;
2. Denying the magnitude of the dollars needed;
3. Waiting for the child to decide on a career;
4. Diverting savings opportunities into consumption items for the child;
5. Thinking someone else will fund their child's education via grants, scholarships and/or loans;
6. Directing too many dollars to overall spending instead of savings;
7. Allowing their children to believe financial resources are unlimited;
8. Taking away a child's partial responsibility for their own education;

9. Believing they can borrow their way out when the time comes;

10. Funding the entire college bill when they should be saving for retirement instead.

Believing that the magic tuition checks will somehow appear at the appropriate time is courting disaster and disappointment. Current consumption levels in many families sap up what could otherwise be an adequate college savings program. With a limited budget under pressure, it might be necessary to turn off the consumption spigot in your home.

Now's the time

This is the time to assess your financial priorities and your responsibility as a parent. Your children might *want* designer jeans, outrageously expensive tennis shoes, and the Nintendo game-of-the-month, but your students *need* college or another higher form of education. If you yield to their demands today for spendable income, how will you tell them tomorrow there is no money for college?

Adolescence, a time of instant gratification, should teach such realities as limited budgets and setting monetary goals. Provide them with the tools for their future.

If you are praying for a miracle because college is right around the corner, the following last-minute options might help:

1. Home equity loans;

2. Perkins (National Direct Student) Loans (NDSL);

3. Guaranteed Student (Stafford) Loans;

4. Supplemental Loans for Students;

5. Parent Loans to Undergraduate Students (PLUS);

6. Loans against life insurance cash values (or withdrawing your money and purchasing term insurance, as you should have all along);

7. A refinanced home mortgage;

8. Retirement employer-plan loans;

9. Retirement plan withdrawals;

10. IRA account terminations;

11. Military programs;

12. Cooperative education;

13. Company-sponsored education;

14. Commuter colleges;

15. Loans against existing securities (for those lucky enough to have some left after the child-raising years).

All of the above programs and emergency plans have disadvantages and should not be used without knowing the "bad news." You can call your local university for more information before researching your options.

If college is less than three years away, don't attempt to achieve a greater return by exposing your funds to greater risks of principal. The primary goal of short-term funds must be the protection of the principal. This means limited investment opportunities such as banks, money markets, investing in U.S. Treasury bills and credit union accounts. Do not be tempted to reach out for greater returns because someone shows you a fancy brochure in the heat of a potential sale.

If you have the time (more than three years) one of my other new books—**MONEY POWER Through Mutual Funds**—will steer you in the right investment direction. For lump-sum investing, I recommend only the dullest and stodgiest of mutual fund types, the equity income "turtles." They make you richer slowly but surely.

Even though long-term marathon money must out-pace inflation, your investments should be built on risk-adverse strategies. If you take greater risks on your precious college funds, you could lose more of your investment principal and still not achieve the goal you sought. The more time you have, the greater the value of compounding becomes. Structure all your long-term assets for comfort, not for speed.

What about prepaid plans?

Wouldn't it be nice for someone to take the risk out of college costs? That's what prepaid college tuition plans and similar programs promise. The proposed benefits sound great: You lock in credits toward a four-year education ahead of time while the trust or management company sweats over how to keep up with rising college costs.

Common sense should trigger some questions. No one can guarantee something that they don't produce—and that goes for well-intentioned programs with optimistic missions. Where would they find the extra funds to make up the difference if they fell short of what they promised? When inflation rates soar, neither stocks nor bonds like the higher atmosphere. Bank deposits usually languish below inflation rates, no matter where they are moving.

"Sorry, we tried," won't substitute for a tuition check at enrollment time. What if the funds are mismanaged? What if your child needs those funds for some other purpose or for medical reasons? What if your child joins the Foreign Legion instead of enrolling in college? Can you get a early refund? How much good will one state's guarantee do you if your student emigrates to another state institution? What accountants and regulators will be watching day and night for inappropriate or risky asset allocation?

Other disadvantages make prepaid programs undesirable. What if your child is not admitted to the school you saved for? You will receive your money back, but perhaps without interest. Someone has to pay taxes on this money you're investing, probably the trust entity. This slows down the annual returns, and at withdrawal time your child might have to pay the taxes on the difference between the actual cost of tuition and the amounts you put in trust.

A better alternative would be to start a regular mutual fund savings program under a tax shelter called the Uniform Gift to Minors Act in your state. Though there are drawbacks to every college funding alternative, this provides real tax relief on an annual basis and more control of the assets and how they are managed.

Chapter 7

On A Clear Day You Can See Retirement

For many families, the challenge of just making it day-to-day overshadows thoughts of planning well into the future. But it would be a mistake to let this attitude discourage you from following a financial plan. The following financial attitudes are just as detrimental:

1. ***What happened to my parents won't happen to me.*** Your parents weren't spendthrifts who shiftlessly mismanaged their paychecks. They were very much like you —immersed in short-term demands, trusting, perhaps intimidated by money, leaving the basic financial decisions up to those who called themselves experts.

They purchased a home as an investment, put their savings into the local bank or S&L, and sent the remainder of their money to insurance companies. Today they may be selling their home to feed themselves and watching helplessly as their fixed-income funds shrink from the annual effects of inflation. Examine your financial position to be sure you aren't traveling down the same dead-end road.

2. ***Conservation of principal should be a retirement plan's top priority.*** That myth is precisely the reason why so many of the elderly desperately need their monthly Social Security checks. The most critical element of any

long-term financial goal must be to protect your *purchasing power*, finding ways to outsmart inflation.

You may be earning 10% on a bank deposit (a dream in this environment), but if inflation is galloping along at 12%, you are *losing* financial ground. Always manage some of your funds for growth.

3. *I will need less money after retirement.* This wishful thought has no foundation. When you retire, you will lose only those monthly mortgage payments and outrageous college tuition bills. You will, however, gain additional health care expenses, increased income taxes from growing social programs, and higher real estate costs. You will likely live longer than today's senior class, have more time to get sick, and face a better chance of outliving your savings.

Inflation won't stop, though your current paycheck will, replaced by a shrinking monthly income of pension and Social Security checks. To survive retirement, you should plan on needing *100%* of what you need to live *today,* increasing at 6% to 10% per year.

4. *I will pay fewer income taxes after retirement.* Paying fewer income taxes many years from now will mean you are in a lower tax bracket than today. Therefore, you will be bringing in less money for living expenses. This may mean fewer meals, not fewer taxes. Think positively: Hope you wind up paying *more* taxes because you have managed to accumulate such a generous retirement fund.

5. *I will have my company pension and Social Security.* Maybe not. As the largest demographic group in history—the baby boomers —gropes toward retirement, not even *our* government might be able to find a way to tax our children enough to subsidize those on the retirement, disabled and indigent rolls.

Corporations are increasingly terminating older workers, attempting to escape the large costs of supporting retirees who will provide no direct benefit to the company's bottom line.

Your retirement income will come from a company pension (if the company is motivated to support you), some Social Security (if your children feel benevolent and are willing to tax themselves even more) and your personal savings. This bleak outlook should motivate you to begin a retirement savings plan now.

6. *It will be easier to save for retirement in a few years.* A growing family will always present financial challenges. With limited finances, growing children and inflation to cope with, depending on future resources is a mistake. There will never be a better time, a cheaper time or a more convenient time to start than now.

The more time your money has to work, the fewer dollars must be spent to achieve your long-term financial goals. A little money worked for a long time at competitive returns will put time on your side.

7. *I'm young, so I have plenty of time.* Time is literally money, and compound interest is the eighth wonder of the world. The top retirement plan in this country today is winning the lottery. Shouldn't you be better prepared?

If it takes $30,000 today after taxes to keep your financial house humming, 12 years from now (at 6% inflation), you'll need $60,000. If you're currently spending $40,000 a year, in 24 years (at the same inflation rate) you'll need $160,000 in today's dollars *just to maintain the same lifestyle*. Where will you get that kind of money unless you start today on a regular retirement savings program?

8. *There will only be the two of us.* Today's boomerang kids are coming back to the roost to continue college, after the death of an underinsured spouse, following a

divorce or as single parents with financial problems. They are also waiting longer (on your paycheck) to marry and set up independent households.

9. *My home is my retirement fund.* This and other fairy tales were exposed during the real estate recession when disappointed homeowners discovered that real estate *can* depreciate. At best, your primary residence will keep pace with inflation. Think of your home as a nest in which to raise your family, not as a shrewd retirement investment.

10. *I'm enjoying my money now while I am young.* There are three basic restrictions on money: (1) the number of years it can compound before you need it; (2) the rate of return or the yield you can receive on your funds; and (3) how much you must share with Uncle Sam in the form of taxes.

The more time you have until retirement, the more awesome the concept of compounding becomes. If you are so bent on living up to the weekly expectations of your entire paycheck, will you be satisfied with fading memories when you reach retirement age?

How to invest for a great retirement

There are many investment vehicles on the market today, but only a few that work better for you than for the salesperson.

If you're like most people, you've been investing in the wrong places. Believing that your money was safely tucked away in the large vault (why else would they hire an armed guard?), you left your dollars in the sanctity of a banking institution.

Or maybe you gave a premium to an insurance company since it was even safer than banks (or so you were told). Your employer's credit union became a short-term storage haven for your funds and even gave you checkwriting privileges. When it offered an automatic payroll deduction, you could pay yourself first and know your money was safe until you needed it.

Americans are a patriotic bunch, and buying U.S. savings bonds was easy because your employer took the money right out of your paycheck. How much safer could money be than backed by the U.S. Government? And you were investing in the "good old U.S. of A."

It never dawned on you that you were loaning out your dollars to these institutions, all of which then invested the money at a significant profit for themselves, then gave you back what was left over.

You knew that the rich invested in other places and bought pieces of companies like Xerox, AT&T and individual bonds. You occasionally read magazine articles about their expert advisors who, for a management fee, handled and managed their assets. But you had only limited funds available. So you stayed where you felt comfortable and where reassuring words like "safe" and "guaranteed" echoed daily through the halls. That was yesterday.

Diversification, simplicity of management, total visibility of your investment via newspaper reporting, and the potential for greater returns are major benefits of mutual fund investing. Funneling your savings through lending institutions or insurance companies just feeds another level of management before your money gets to the actual investment. You will have challenge enough racing against time and inflation without contributing a share of your profits to someone else's retirement plan.

Today you can pool your funds with large and other small investors, hire a top money manager to purchase securities for you, enjoy the benefits of volume buying and keep a larger share of the earnings for yourself. An investment advisor (either an individual or a team) will assume the duties of active management as well as the daily responsibilities for investment decisions. They will manage your portfolio on a full-time basis.

You can choose a portfolio manager with the same basic investment philosophy, limit the investing methods and strategies they can use, and direct other important investment policies. Since you do other things well, you can turn over the active management responsibilities to those trained in this arena.

Mutual funds are sold directly to you by investment companies or through financial intermediaries such as banks, insurance companies, financial service corporations and brokerages. I recommend you conduct your own research before contacting any of the above retailers, especially a sales agent whose own self-interest in the heat of passion for a sale may outweigh any concern for your welfare.

You can choose from a litter of nearly 3,700 individual funds, not including those issued by insurance companies and a few isolated organizations. Track your favorites using the advice in **MONEY POWER Through Mutual Funds.**

Avoid insurance products advertised as IRA alternatives. They are insurance policies dressed up to look like attractive investment vehicles. Their returns are dismal due to the heavy expenses, charges and commissions extracted. Insurance annuities are not much more helpful and are inflexible, outmoded and expensive retirement vehicles.

Tax-advantaged company pension plans such as 401ks, thrift savings programs or deferred compensation programs should be investigated first for the quality of the underlying investment vehicle before grabbing the tax shelter tag. It makes a difference whether you are investing in pygmy bonds, Tasmanian devils or a high-quality mutual fund.

How to become a millionaire

It may be more beneficial to limit your company savings (even with the tax gimmicks and a company match) and find a more suitable investment vehicle. An IRA, whether you have a company pension or not, should be in your Christmas stocking each and every year.

A $2,000 annual investment from age 22 until age 67 working at 10% per year will grow into $1,581,591. If the return can be increased to 12% per year, the total accumulation at age 67 would be $3,042,435. Now for the bad news: Those figures do not reflect any taxes you may pay on an annual basis. The IRA to the rescue!

An IRA account (wrapped around a mutual fund investment) will shelter your profits from yearly taxes until you withdraw your money after retirement. If you are in a 15% tax bracket, a taxable 10% return means you actually only earn 8.5%. So without the IRA label, your potential savings of $1,581,591 shrink to $977,651. Even a 12% return will suffer due to current taxation, accumulating only $1,687,554 compared with its potential of $3,042,435 without the tax man. By adding the IRA label to your $2,000 mutual fund investment, you can say goodbye to taxes until retirement time.

In the 28% tax bracket, the effects are even more startling. A 10% return taxed at 28% yields only 7.2% per year, total savings at age 67 of only $650,455 instead of $1,581,591. Increasing your rate of return to 12% helps. But the IRA account grows yearly *without shrinkage,* while the taxable account is at the mercy of the tax man.

None of these examples include additional benefits you might receive from IRA investing. If you can deduct part or all of your annual IRA contribution, your money will grow even faster.

A small amount of money, worked over a long period of time at a competitive rate without current taxation, is very powerful. Inflation will seriously erode your purchasing power. So choose a high quality mutual fund and start your retirement planning today.

And for answers to all your IRA questions, see the next chapter.

If your company retires first

If you retire, become disabled or change employment, you may have the option to leave your pension fund with your company, take it to your new employer or roll it over into an IRA account and invest it yourself.

Your retirement dollars are the most important you will ever produce. A stranger has been investing your nest egg for years, most likely without your knowledge of where and how well it was managed. If the company offers a lump-sum option, consider taking charge of your own assets.

You have nothing more important to do than watch over your own retirement pot. Diversify it into a combination of bank deposits, a money market mutual fund that invests only in U.S. Government issues, and those dull, boring and stodgy mutual fund "turtles," the equity income types. Perhaps you can add the seasoning of a global fund. Again, **MONEY POWER Through Mutual Funds** can help you invest like the pros—perhaps even better. Even the best money managers lose someone else's money sometimes.

Choosing a monthly income option instead of the one-time lump sum election may limit your freedom to change your mind later. What if you need medical care your health insurance won't cover? How will you handle a large unexpected financial crisis? Maybe you will want a few extra days with your grandkids.

Such an irrevocable step just adds another monthly check for inflation to eat away at. With projected health care costs at astronomical levels, you will need the flexibility to take your money as you see fit, when you need it.

What will happen if your company disappears during your retirement? How will you cope if the promises made to retirees and their families become greater than pension assets can produce? As more and more workers consider longer retirements, long-term pension promises are tremendous risks, especially if you have no seat on the company's board of directors and no golden executive parachute.

Occasionally, a company's lump-sum offer is so paltry compared to the monthly income option that you have little choice but to take the latter.

Before you make a final election that could be irrevocable, get a tax advisor or real financial planner to calculate the lump-sum potential at a current interest rate invested by you and paid out over your lifetime. Compare these figures with the monthly payment retirement plan.

This number-crunching is vital and should not be combined with your purchase of any financial product or investment. Get only the figures you need; avoid all sales pitches you may encounter. It is dangerous to your financial health to dangle a large retirement pot in front of a hungry product vendor. Money may calm the nerves, but it also attracts the vultures.

Chapter 8

Bring Back Your IRA Account

When Congress eliminated the tax deductibility of Individual Retirement Account (IRA) contributions for people with employer-sponsored retirement programs, they inadvertently sent the wrong message to these consumers: Stop investing in IRAs. Despite the fact that many people can no longer deduct the value of their contributions, IRAs remain one of the best long-term investments you can make—provided, of course, they are comprised of sound investment vehicles.

In this chapter, we will tackle some of the most frequently asked questions about IRAs.

Q: What is an Individual Retirement Account (IRA)?

It's not a stock, a bond or a bank CD. It is a special tax shelter set up by Congress for retirement savings. You can invest in a variety of investments and tack on the IRA tax shelter label. All earnings in an IRA account are tax-deferred until you withdraw them at retirement time (or sooner, if you wish). And for many of you, annual contributions are *still* tax-deductible right now.

Q: Who can open an IRA?

Anyone age 70 or younger who earns a paycheck can contribute to an IRA. It doesn't matter how long you have worked, whether your company has a retirement plan of its own, or how many other employers you have worked for during the year.

Rents, royalties and income from investments do *not* qualify. Alimony, however, *is* considered income for IRA purposes. If you work for a living, you are eligible.

Q: My company has both a pension and a 401k retirement plan. Can I still contribute to an IRA?

Absolutely. Even if you think you will have adequate retirement funding, it makes sense to contribute annually to an IRA account. Some company pensions have gone bankrupt and many will be overburdened by the liabilities of future retirees and their families.

If you have too much money at retirement, you can always donate some to one of the millions of Americans who will have too little.

Q: How much money can I contribute to an IRA?

Every year you can put away a maximum of $2,000. If you earn less than $2,000 a year, you can contribute all of your earnings if you wish. Non-working spouses can also have a spousal IRA of $250 per year. That equals a total of $2,250 per couple, which can be split in any way as long as neither spouse claims more than $2,000.

Q. Do I get a tax break right away?

In many cases, yes. If you or your spouse are not active participants in any company pension plan or are not eligible for one, the amount you earn does not matter. You may deduct off your taxes the full $2,000, even if you made $100,000.

If you are a single person eligible for or participating in a company pension who earns more than $25,000 in one year, you will be limited to how much of the IRA contribution you can deduct. There is a reduction of 10% for every $1,000 you earn above $25,000.

For example, if you earned $30,000, you would be able to write off only $1,000 of the $2,000 contribution or 50% of whatever you contributed if that amount is less. If you made $35,000, you cannot deduct any of your IRA contribution.

If you're married, the deduction phases out at higher limits. For couples with a company pension plan (or if one or both are eligible even though they don't participate), income above $40,000 proportionately discreases the deductibility of the IRA contribution. Above $50,000 adjusted gross income, none of the IRA contribution can be deducted.

The tax deduction is the primary reason so many Americans began IRA accounts. In a 15% federal tax bracket, you could save $300 in taxes by saying those magic letters "IRA." That extra $300 was a return on the $1,700 you could have kept if the money had been immediately taxed. A $300 profit on $1,700 is a 17.6% return, without even considering the compounding power of a competitive investment year after year.

In a 28% tax bracket, the results are even more powerful. Without an IRA, you would retain only $1,440 (of the $2,000 potential IRA contribution), while your $560 in taxes was distributed elsewhere. An IRA may allow you to claim back that $560, saving you that much in taxes and giving you an immediate profit of 38.9%.

Many workers cannot deduct part or any of their IRA contributions anymore. But as we shall see, the power of tax-deferral is just as awesome. Even a non-deductible IRA should be seriously considered.

Q: Besides the immediate tax deduction, what other tax benefits does an IRA provide?

You don't pay taxes on any earnings until retirement time or age 70 1/2 (if you choose to leave money sheltered for that long). You lose the amazing potential of tax-deferred profits and the tragic opportunity costs as each year goes by without your annual IRA contribution.

Whether you can deduct all, part or none of your IRA investment, diligently use it. An IRA is like eating spinach: It's good for you, even if you can't immediately understand why.

Q: Will I get any tax advantages when I retire?

At age 59 1/2 but no later than age 70 1/2, you will start withdrawing without penalty and paying taxes on some of your IRA assets. If you don't need to, take out only what is required by law. The longer your dollars work inside a tax shelter, the harder they can work. You don't *have* to withdraw any IRA money until age 70 1/2.

Until that time, you can keep your IRA sheltered from the clutches of the taxman. When you are finally taxed, IRA withdrawals will be treated like the rest of your regular income.

Q: What if I can't invest the whole $2,000 each year?

Most mutual funds allow a minimum investment of as little as $25 a month into an IRA account (or a lump sum as little as $250). Save whatever you can. There is no minimum that must be contributed on an annual basis. By systematic investing, even small amounts can build into a sizable nest egg over time. Time is the key element to working your money, along with, of course, a reasonable rate of return. That's why so many small investors choose the greater profit potential of mutual funds for their retirement IRA accounts.

Q: Must I save the same amount every year?

There are no requirements on the amount you must contribute. If you have a good year, max out your IRA. When times are not so good, invest what you can. You can skip years, then start investing again. You decide when and how much to invest.

Q: How do I open an IRA with a mutual fund?

All funds have special IRA applications. The procedure is as simple as opening up any other kind of investment account. Remember, though, that IRA accounts have special tax rules you need to understand before sending money to the mutual fund you've chosen.

Q: Is there a deadline for putting money into an IRA?

You may contribute to an IRA each year until April 15 of the following year. If you file your taxes at the last minute, be sure your IRA contribution is safely tucked away in a mutual fund by midnight on April 15 for the previous tax year.

If you get an extension for filing your tax return, you must still make your IRA contribution by April 15—the regular deadline for filing your taxes—in order to claim the prior year's deduction.

Q: Should I wait until the end of the year to make a contribution to my IRA?

The more time your money has to work, the more powerful it becomes. The longer your money works without sharing it with Uncle Sam, the more you can keep over the long run. So depositing $2,000 on January 1 of your new tax year is ideal. But many folks are recovering from Christmas or have no savings plan for this purpose.

If you invest $166.66 on a monthly basis starting in January, you will have some money working for you throughout the year, and the full $2,000 invested by December.

The least beneficial, but better than not contributing at all, is the last-minute IRA, just before tax time.

If you make any contributions during the year, all earnings on your investment will grow tax-free. In this case, time really is money.

Q: Can I split up an IRA into different types of investments?

You can split up an IRA contribution any way you wish. In fact, I recommend that you search for at least two mutual funds with different investment objectives. That way you can diversify among more than one type of investment and accommodate a larger investment menu.

For example, you may want to invest most of your IRA money in a conservative mutual fund and the remainder in a global fund for greater diversification.

Q: If I don't contribute the full amount one year, can I make up the balance another year?

No. But remember, you have until April 15 of the following year to make *last* year's IRA contribution. Always fill up the prior year's IRA before starting on the current year's contribution.

Q: What happens if I accidentally put too much into my IRA account and contribute more than my limit in one year?

If this happens, you can remove any excess by con-tacting your mutual fund for specific instructions. If you remove the extra money before you file your tax return, you won't be penalized.

If you are too late, the excess can be transferred to next year's account. However, you will be taxed 6% on the excess contribution in the meantime. Watch your regular fund statements, which tell you exactly how much money you have invested.

If you are sending your IRA to more than one fund at a time, be sure to watch both statements so you don't contribute too much. No matter how many types of IRA investments you own, the maximum amount you can invest for one tax year is $2,000 per person or 100% of your earned income, whichever is less.

Q: What if I don't have enough money left over from my earnings to contribute to an IRA account?

You can use any money—your savings, a general investment in a mutual fund or money from a credit union—it doesn't have to be the same money you earned. The only requirement is that you must have earned that much income to be eligible for an IRA account.

Q: Can my spouse and I both have an IRA account if only one of us works?

Yes. This is called a spousal IRA account. A total of $2,250 can be contributed annually as long as one spouse does not contribute more than $2,000 of the total amount in his or her name.

Q: I am divorced and do not work. Can I open an IRA account?

For IRA purposes, alimony is considered as income. So you can contribute to an IRA up to $2,000 or 100% of any alimony received, whichever is less.

Q: I am self-employed and have a SEP (or KEOGH). Am I also entitled to an IRA?

Yes, you can open both a SEP (or KEOGH) and an IRA account. The IRA may not be tax-deductible, but you should contribute anyway. The more money you can shelter, one way or another, the better.

Q: Can my employer contribute to an IRA for me?

Yes. Many small companies create simplified pensions in this manner for their employees. The forms to be filed are minimal, and the plan is inexpensive to administer. Employers can contribute totally and exclusively to such a plan or employees can also contribute through a payroll deduction plan. Each employee has a separate investment account with all the privileges of a regular IRA account.

Q: What happens to my IRA account if my spouse and I get a divorce?

A divorce should not affect the tax-deferred status of your IRA. It may, however, be considered marital property for property settlement purposes. If you transfer part or all of your IRA to your spouse during a divorce settlement, the IRA tax shelter can remain in effect for both you and for your spouse. Consult a tax attorney to advise you in this matter.

Q: May I use my IRA account as collateral for a personal or business loan?

You may *not* use your IRA for *any* borrowing purposes. If you do, it will be considered an immediate distribution, and all taxes will be immediately due in the year you engage in such a transaction.

Q: When can I withdraw my IRA account?

You can withdraw your money at any time, but if you are under age 59 1/2 and have not died or been disabled, you will incur a 10% penalty for early withdrawal *plus* pay taxes on whatever amount you withdraw.

You can begin withdrawals from an IRA with*out* any penalty after age 59 1/2. You don't *need* to start withdrawing from your IRA account until the April following the year you turn 70 1/2.

Q: How do I direct my IRA account to my heirs?

The simplest method is by naming them as beneficiaries. On your IRA mutual fund application, you will find spaces for a primary beneficiary (the first person who receives the money if you die) and for a contingent or secondary beneficiary (who will receive your assets if the primary beneficiary is not living).

In this way, your IRA account will go directly to your heirs and avoid probate. However, only a spouse is eligible to roll over the money to his or her own IRA.

Q: How is the money I withdraw taxed?

Your tax-deferred profits and all contributions which were not taxed when they were contributed will be treated like interest from a CD or any other type of investment income. However, you pay taxes only on the amount you withdraw in any one year. The remainder of your IRA account remains tax-deferred until you withdraw it.

Q: What if I retire before age 59 1/2 and need supplemental income from my IRA account?

You may withdraw a substantially equal amount each year from your IRA account without penalty based on your future life expectancy. You will pay the taxes on your money but will *not* incur the 10% IRA early-withdrawal penalty.

This is a complicated process and should not be attempted without the assistance of a tax advisor, a financial planner or someone from the IRS. Once you start this process, you must continue taking the annual withdrawals for at least 5 years or to age 59 1/2, whichever period is longer.

Q: All my IRAs are with banks and insurance companies. Can I move them into mutual funds?

Your insurance annuity can be transferred by requesting an account surrender in writing. If you are told you will incur severe surrender charges by moving now, realize that any such charges are investment expenses charged when you originally invested. That money is already gone—into the pockets of both the agent and the company. You opted for the free lunch, believing that someone would invest your money for nothing, and these internal charges are coming back to haunt you.

You have only 60 days from the date you receive your check to roll over your savings into another investment. If you miss your 60-day transfer deadline, you will lose the IRA tax benefit and all money will become taxable in that year.

You will probably want to wait until your CD matures to roll over your savings into a mutual fund. Otherwise, you may incur early withdrawal penalties. Many lending institutions currently offer penalty-free withdrawals for senior citizens. Ask your bank about withdrawal privileges and penalties.

Q: What records should I keep?

Copy everything for your files, including the IRA mutual fund application and both front and back of every check. This documents a clear paper trail in case the IRS should question any of your contributions or transfers at a later time. Always send important documentation via certified mail, return receipt requested.

Keep IRA rollover accounts separate from other mutual fund money, even if you invest all your savings in the same mutual fund. I recommend keeping IRA roll-over money and new annual IRA contributions in separate accounts also. The better the paper trail, the easier it will be to defend your actions in ten or fifteen years if there should be any question.

Q: How often can I change my IRA account to another investment vehicle?

If you had nothing better to do, you could transfer from place to place on a daily basis. However, tax law only allows one check sent directly to you each 365 days. To transfer more often, simply request a direct transfer of funds to the new investment company or mutual fund.

Q: If I can't deduct my IRA contributions, why should I bother ?

Suppose a taxpayer makes an annual $2,000 *totally non-deductible* IRA contribution at the beginning of each year, as opposed to merely investing $2,000 per year in a taxable investment. Both the non-deductible IRA and the taxable investment capital are invested in the same investment vehicle, whose return averages 10% per year. But the IRA has the advantage of tax-deferred profits year after year. The following is the result of each investment at the end of 20 and 30 years:

At the end of:	Non-deductible IRA	Taxable Investment*
20 years	$126,005	$ 84,272
30 years	$361,887	$189,588

* I have assumed our taxpayer is in the 28% marginal tax bracket and 5% state and local income tax brackets.

The longer the period of time that money can compound, the larger the gap between the IRA account and the taxable investments. Remember: No contributions to the IRA account shown above are immediately tax deductible—only the benefits of tax-*deferred* compounding are seen here. If any portion of the IRA account can be deducted, the advantages over time will be even greater.

Q: How long must I keep my IRA account records?

For the rest of your life or eternity, whichever is longer. Most mutual funds provide a year-end statement that summarizes the year's activities. In addition, many also send cost-basis statements so you can easily figure which shares you sold and how much they originally cost.

If the IRS should ever doubt your reporting, the burden of proof is on you. There are significant penalties and nasty tax consequences for lack of data. If you own a combination of tax-deductible, partially deductible and non-deductible IRAs, don't depend on your memory or any institution's records to keep track.

Q: Where can I get additional information regarding how IRA accounts work and the laws affecting them?

Most mutual funds have a comprehensive informational packet that you can order. There usually is a lot of fine print, but you can get a clearer understanding of intricate regulations that cannot be discussed here.

Chapter 9

Learning The Lingo
Of The Pros

According to one of my favorite jokes, if you laid all the economists in the world end to end, they couldn't reach a conclusion.

Nevertheless, economists' lingo rules the financial world—and our lives!

For instance, we've been hearing about a recession for two years now. It's caused businesses to slow down, has probably caused you to be more cautious with your money, has even moved a President out of office. But how many of us can explain what the word "recession" means?

In this chapter, we'll somewhat lightheartedly examine some economic terms and translate them into terms that all of us can understand.

RECESSION: A slowdown or slump in the nation's leading indicators for more than two consecutive quarters. Examples of leading indicators are the consumer price index, interest rates, home starts and the sale of retail goods and services.

DEPRESSION: A prolonged period of recession marked by massive unemployment, a major reduction in business production and a great number of personal and corporate bankruptcies. Consumer confidence is low, and spending has slowed considerably.

Translation: A recession is when someone you know is out of work. A depression is when *you* are out of work.

UPSWING IN THE ECONOMY: Corporate profits are on the rise, and business is beginning to borrow healthy amounts of money for expansion. Leading indicators are up, unemployment is down.

Translation: Your paycheck rises enough to add one more monthly credit payment.

GOVERNMENTAL MONETARY POLICY: Bureaucratic policies and federal programs ease or restrict the money supply and assist smooth transitions through the various stages of the business cycle.

Translation: Monetary policy should not be confused with fiscal policy, as your government has no money to make policy with except *yours* (which it systematically takes). Monetary policy in any one direction rarely lasts more than 90 days, the time when the next popularity poll is taken.

TIGHT-MONEY OR EASY-MONEY POLICY: A concerted effort is made by the Federal Reserve to hold down interest rates and promote borrowing to stimulate an economic recovery. As expansion develops into full-blown prosperity, credit is purposely restricted, reducing the money supply, driving up interest rates and staving off inflationary pressures.

Translation: *Tight money* is a well-known middle-class phenomenon, meaning there is more month left at the end of the money. *Easy money* is what your teenagers think you are made of. Some families and their money are living so far apart that they are practically strangers. Most families practice primarily tight-money policies (at least until the kids are all out of college).

DISCOUNT RATE: The price that large lenders pay for money, which they then sell to their customers. When this rate is low, lenders' costs decrease so they can, in turn, pass on that good news to their customers in the form of higher returns and lower costs for borrowed money.

Translation: If CD and savings account rates go any lower, I intend to donate my money and take a charitable deduction off my taxes. Today's rates give new meaning to the words "get rich slow."

PRIME RATE: The prevailing interest rate at which money is loaned out to a lender's best customers.

Translation: You, however, are not on that list. You can buy only one house and have enough paycheck left over for only two car payments. You are the little guy, the loyal customer who keeps lenders in business, paying your mortgages quietly and dependably each month when the big customers like AT&T and the Rockefellers are not hanging around the bank's office. The prime rate has little real meaning for you, the average consumer.

THE COST OF MONEY: The prevailing interest rate is the price of money. This cost fluctuates according to the laws of supply and demand. When these natural forces don't work properly, the Fed (Federal Reserve) tampers by buying or selling securities from lenders, thereby increasing or reducing bank reserves. This process adds to or reduces an institution's ability to lend.

Translation: Money is like a lawn mower or a toaster—it comes at different prices, and you should shop for it just as you buy soap and poultry at your supermarket. When you are loaning yours to others, seek the highest returns. When borrowing theirs, negotiate for the cheapest rate you can find.

TOTAL GROSS COMPENSATION: The sum total of all wages and benefits a worker receives, including health care, disability insurance, pension plans and vacation or sick leave is called the economic cost of an employee to his or her company.

Translation: You never see your *gross* pay. It's a meaningless number, what your boss tries to convince you the company is shelling out for you. You never see gross, you can't spend gross and you don't manage gross. Only *take-home* pay is meaningful—that's what you have to spend.

INFLATION: Too many dollars chasing too few goods is the standard definition. When demand exceeds supply at current prices, those prices are bid up.

Translation: Your last car cost more than your first house. Motel 6, now Motel $29.95, may be Motel $75 by the time you retire. Inflation is *not* an economic concept; it is by far the deadliest money-killer over long periods of time.

Inflation will *never* go away. It must be planned for, because by the time you discover its symptoms, you have become its victim. Always manage your money for some growth to consistently outpace inflation.

CONSUMER PRICE INDEX (CPI): The CPI represents a mythical basket of goods and services designed to compare relative price changes over time. Many benefits, such as pension cost-of-living raises, Social Security increases and entitlement programs, are linked to the CPI.

Translation: Whoever makes up this universal basket of expenses you are supposedly purchasing isn't checking out your grocery receipts, last month's electric bills, the cost of your health care insurance or your student's tuition invoices. Plan for inflation hikes of close to 6%, not the comforting figures propagandists are publishing.

TREASURY BILLS (T-BILLS): Short-term investments (debt obligations) are issued by the U.S. Treasury on a discount basis (you pay a little less than their face value of $10,000). Treasury bills constitute a large portion of our national debt, and this huge dollar volume is considered the bellweather of short-term interest throughout the economy. The most frequent reason for purchasing T-bills is to earn short-term interest on idle cash.

Translation: Most consumers have such limited idle funds that purchasing one security at a price of $10,000 per bill is as likely for them as placing in the Kentucky Derby without the aid of a horse.

NATIONAL BUDGET DEFICIT: The accounting shortfall resulting from government spending (borrowing) more than it takes in. The deficit is currently over $4 *trillion*.

Translation: When numbers get that large, we lose all track of their impact and horror. We also lose the confidence to tackle such a mountain of debt and get back into the black, to run our government the way we must run our own budgets. If we, as consumers and spenders, must have it all today, our children and their children will pay for it tomorrow...and tomorrow...and tomorrow.

LEADING ECONOMIC INDICATORS: Signs are utilized to predict changes in the business cycle, similar to a meteorologist's barometer. Examples include first-time unemployment claims, manufacturers' new orders for goods and materials, new building permits and the money supply.

Translation: The middle-class has its own set of indicators, which seem even better omens of what's ahead: The paycheck doesn't go as far as it used to, the emergency fund is shrinking, savings are decreasing, over-time is being cut down, and the second-family income has collapsed. During good economic times, the reverse may be true. But it has been so long since we had a growing economy that I can't, for the life of me, remember what those signs are.

BUSINESS CYCLE: A continual transition from trough (recession) to recovery.
Translation: Whatever comes up must go down.

PROSPECTUS: A document that provides information about a mutual fund to potential buyers.
Translation: The bold print giveth while the fine print taketh away. (But what small investor can read either?) If you can thoughtfully analyze a prospectus, you don't need one.

I figure if the mutual fund company wanted folks to know what was happening to their money, they would print the darned things in plain English instead of alien terms that bore you to tears before you get to the second paragraph.

SINKING FUND: A pool of money that provides for the orderly retirement of a bond issue during its life.
Translation: Last year's top consumer mutual fund that you purchased and have been watching slowly lose investment principal ever since. Hindsight may be 20/20, but your investment returns depend on p-r-o-f-i-t-s, not p-r-o-p-h-e-t-s! The small investor buys high and sells low. Learn to think like the rich: Buy low and sell high.

BULL MARKET: An extended period of time when the stock market rises sharply. It is traditionally accompanied by investor optimism and confidence, easy credit and economic recovery. During this period, the quality of securities is secondary to the momentum and direction of the market in general. Investors snap up lower quality issues, often bidding them up unrealistically due to some ill-founded euphoria.
Translation: There are three types of financial investors: those who *make* things happen, such as large institutional traders who take risks first and reap the greatest profits (or losses); those who *watch* things happen, such

as small investors who sit on the sidelines and never get into the game; and those who *keep wondering what happened,* such as other small investors who jump in for the wrong reasons at the wrong time, buying high and selling low.

BEAR MARKET: A period when the stock market declines rapidly with no relief in sight. Historically, bear markets have lasted as long as 18 months. Most issues suffer price deterioration, and even defensive stocks (those too stubborn to lie down at first) finally lose value.

Bear markets are characterized by public pessimism, lack of investor confidence and economic downturn. The government may institute fiscal and monetary policy supports to soften such a landing. Savings are high, and consumer spending becomes restrained.

Translation: Lacking the knowledge to avoid such roller-coaster rides, and without the discipline to hang on through the worst, novices flee back to the safety of lending institutions. Safety becomes more important than yield, and the investor loses the next opportunity to make money in the stock market rally that follows.

The bulls make money, and the bears can even glean a profit during the bad times. But the piggies get slaughtered. You must take all the animals out of your personal investing philosophy so you have less manure to wade through on your journey. Never invest out of greed or run away out of fear.

BLUE CHIP STOCKS: These are stocks in companies with long records of earnings, dividends and competent management, mature corporations with stable earnings histories that are household names. Investors tend to pay higher prices for these companies, which symbolize greater safety of investment capital.

Translation: During the crash of 1987, these stalwart veterans lost more value than "riskier" types of stocks. The following day there was a "22% Off" sale on such gems as GE, AT&T and Eastman Kodak. There is no such thing as a safe stock. All stocks move up and down and are too risky for small investors. S-A-F-E is a four-letter word and a great big lie. Structure your portfolio for comfort, not for speed and follow the three fundamental rules of investing: (1) diversify; (2) diversify; and (3) diversify.

BONDS: Long-term debt represents a contractual obligation by the issuer to pay interest and/or principal. Bonds can be issued by the federal government, by private corporations, even by cities, states and revenue projects (such as toll roads, airports and public works). Some bonds are taxable; others may be partially or totally tax-free.

Translation: Bonds are believed to be "safer" investments than stocks, which some investors fear more than psoriasis. All bonds, however, move up and down according to what interest rates are doing. In 1987 (April and again in June), general interest rates moved up 2%, while bond investors unwittingly lost 20% of their principal, whether they realized it or not. "Safe" long-term U.S. Government bonds have price volatility over long periods of time, because time is a risk. Generally, the longer the time to maturity, the greater the risk to principal.

Risk is everywhere. You cannot avoid it, but you can learn to manage risk through intelligent diversification and conservative investing policies. If it sounds too good to be true, it probably is.

TOTAL RETURN: The total profit (or loss) from an investment for a given time period, including both yield and the gain or loss of principal. It may be stated as an annual effective yield or a compound rate of return.

Translation: There are two elements to every investment: the yield and the effect on investment principal. Too many fixed-income vehicles provide a great yield at the expense of shrinking principal. If that price per share goes down, you are losing investment capital. Put simply: Be sure to get not only a return *on* your money but also a return *of* your money.

DOW JONES INDUSTRIAL AVERAGE: The best known index, it has little relation to the stock market as a whole. It tracks only the stock movements of 30 industrial companies that have changed composition greatly since the Dow's inception.

Translation: Discussing the Dow will ingratiate you at cocktail parties and give the impression that you are an astute financial mind, worthy of attracting a small group of onlookers and information seekers. As a tool to understanding financial markets, however, it is relatively inane, as it bounces up and down according to the purchasing habits of only a small segment of investors.

STANDARD AND POOR'S 500 COMPOSITE INDEX: This average tracks 500 companies, a broader base for visualizing stock market trends. It is weighted for size and for stock splits. Its individual companies produce everything from ant poison to zippers. Therefore, it reflects a better picture of what's happening to industry.

Translation: If you are looking for a crystal ball, this index gives a broader picture of where the market has been, if not where it is going tomorrow.

NASDAQ COMPOSITE INDEX: The average price of approximately 5,000 over-the-counter issues, mostly newer, riskier companies with small capitalizations but bright futures.

Translation: This is the "now you see it, now you don't" index. As dangerous as shark-infested waters, this is no place for the uninitiated. Even the experts lose big with these high fliers. Don't let the altitude of some exceptional performances cloud your common sense. Manage your wealth as you would your business—carefully.

CERTIFICATE OF DEPOSIT: A time deposit savings account that pays a fixed yield over the specific period of time the money must be left with the lender. Most CDs are protected by the Federal Deposit Insurance Corporation (FDIC) against loss of principal. There is usually a significant penalty for withdrawing a CD before its maturity date.

Translation: A CD is also a Certificate of Depreciation. Of all the guarantees lenders offer, the one they fail to disclose is the guaranteed loss of real principal over time due to inflation. If you put all your assets into CDs, you may go broke...safely.

RISK: The chance that the actual return on an investment will be different from the expected return.

Translation: Risk is a term the small investor does not understand. Lured by fat double-digit returns (from prior-year performances), investors often unknowingly choose high-risk investments.

The careful investor is risk-adverse, an investment wimp. Folks have been taught that greater risks will reap bigger profits; in today's market, higher risk means only greater potential loss of principal. Markets are merciless, and intrepid novices unknowingly take chances that even a fighter pilot would avoid. *The more risk you take with your money, the more of it you will eventually lose.*

The major difference between a paranoid and a realist is that the paranoid *thinks* the world is after him, while the realist knows it! It's a jungle out there. Be a realist.

TAX SHELTERS: Some investments can create either tax-deductible benefits, tax-deferred profits, tax-free income or all of the above for their owners.

Translation: Folks will do nearly anything to avoid paying taxes, even lose money. Tax-advantaged investments can be inferior vehicles and far from safe. Tax planning should be the *last* consideration, not a primary investment objective.

Translation of this entire chapter: Don't listen to the economists and the pundits. Use your common sense and get a good financial education. Then, go and manage your investments yourself.

Index